OKSANA
BAIUL

(Photo on front cover.)

Oksana Baiul celebrates her gold medal performance in the 1993 World Figure Skating Championships.

(Photo on previous pages.)

Baiul, center, on the podium with Surya Bonaly of France, left, and Lu Chen of China.

Library of Congress Cataloging-in-Publication Data
Rambeck, Richard.
Oksana Baiul / Richard Rambeck.
p. cm.
Summary: A biography of young skater who won a gold medal at the 1994 Winter Olympics.
ISBN 1-56766-205-6
1. Baiul, Oksana, 1977 or 8- —Juvenile literature.
2. Skaters—Ukraine—Biography—Juvenile literature.
 [1. Baiul, Oksana, 1977 or 8- 2. Ice Skaters.]
 I. Title

GV850.B35R36 1995   95-7290
796.91'092—dc20   CIP
  [B]   AC

OKSANA
BAIUL

BY RICHARD RAMBECK

Every time Oksana Baiul moved, her back hurt. The 16-year-old figure skater from the Ukraine was in a position to win a gold medal. The finals of the women's figure skating competition at the 1994 Winter Olympics in Lillehammer, Norway, were only a few hours away. Baiul, however, was wondering if she would get a chance to skate. The pain in her back was terrible. How could she possibly do the jumps she needed to do on the ice?

The day before the figure skating finals, Oksana was practicing on the ice rink in Hamar, Norway. Suddenly, Baiul and a skater from Germany ran into each other. Both fell to the ice. Baiul had a cut on her shin. But the real problem was her back. Oksana was in second place after the first round of the competition. She trailed U.S. skater Nancy Kerrigan by only a few points. Oksana could win the gold—but she needed to be healthy to do it.

I n the morning before the final round, Baiul took painkillers. She and her coach, Galina Zmievskaya, knew that if the painkillers didn't work, Oksana probably wouldn't be able to skate. It would have been so sad for her to get this close to Olympic greatness and not be able to compete. If she hadn't been

Baiul ends her Olympic short program in Hamar, Norway.

able to skate—it would have been another sad chapter in Baiul's life. This time, though, her story would have a happy ending.

O ksana Baiul was born in Dnepropetrovsk, an industrial city in the central part of the Ukraine. The Ukraine, which is located in Eastern Europe, was then part of the Soviet Union. But the country gained its independence when the Soviet Union broke up in 1992. When Oksana was two, her father left home, never to return. Still, she got plenty of love from her mother and grandparents. Young Oksana dreamed of being a ballerina.

But Baiul wasn't as thin as the other girls who took ballet lessons. She wasn't really built for ballet back then. Her grandfather bought her a pair of ice skates, and Oksana decided she would try to become a ballerina on ice. Baiul skated and skated. Soon, it became clear she was a natural talent. But her world at home was about to fall apart. When Oksana was 13, her mother died of cancer. Her parents were both gone.

Soon after her mother's death, Oksana suffered another loss. Her longtime coach, Stanislav Koretek, left the Ukraine and moved to Canada.

Baiul performs a lighthearted exhibition.

Before he left, Koretek found Oksana a new coach. In 1992, he called Zmievskaya and asked her to take the young skater under her wing. Zmievskaya knew how to mold Olympic champions. She had coached Ukrainian men's star Victor Petrenko to the gold medal in the 1992 Winter Olympics.

Zmievskaya agreed to coach Baiul. Oksana moved to Zmievskaya's home in Odessa, a city in the southern part of the Ukraine on the Black Sea. Zmievskaya became Oksana's coach and guardian. "The skating world is now her family," Zmievskaya said. But it was a poor family. The ice rink in Odessa

15

where Baiul trained was bumpy and filled with watery spots in places. It was hardly a place to develop an Olympic champion.

Petrenko, who also trained at the same ice rink in Odessa, helped Oksana by buying her ice skates and skating outfits. Meanwhile, despite the poor conditions of the ice, Baiul continued to improve. "It's all natural to her," Zmievskaya said. "You tell her something, and she goes, 'Like this?' She does it all on her own." Oksana herself called her skating ability "a gift from God" and said, "I skate how I feel."

In January 1993, Baiul entered her first international competition, the European figure skating championships. Nobody had ever heard of the tiny Ukrainian skater. That would soon change. She finished second, an incredible performance in her first major competition. In March 1993, the 15-year-old Oksana traveled to Prague, Czechoslovakia, for the world championships. She shocked everyone by winning the competition.

At the 1994 Winter Olympics, Oksana was given a good chance to win a medal, perhaps even a gold medal. She was second to Nancy

Kerrigan after the first round. But the accident during practice put her medal hopes in doubt. The painkillers she took for her aching back worked. She would compete in the finals. Kerrigan skated before Baiul in the finals and turned in a superb performance.

Now it was Oksana's turn. When her name was called, she did what she always does before skating onto the ice. She waited several seconds. Why? "I listen to my skates," she said. "When they can start, they go to the start." Baiul listened to her skates, and then went out and gave the performance of her life. She was like a magician on the

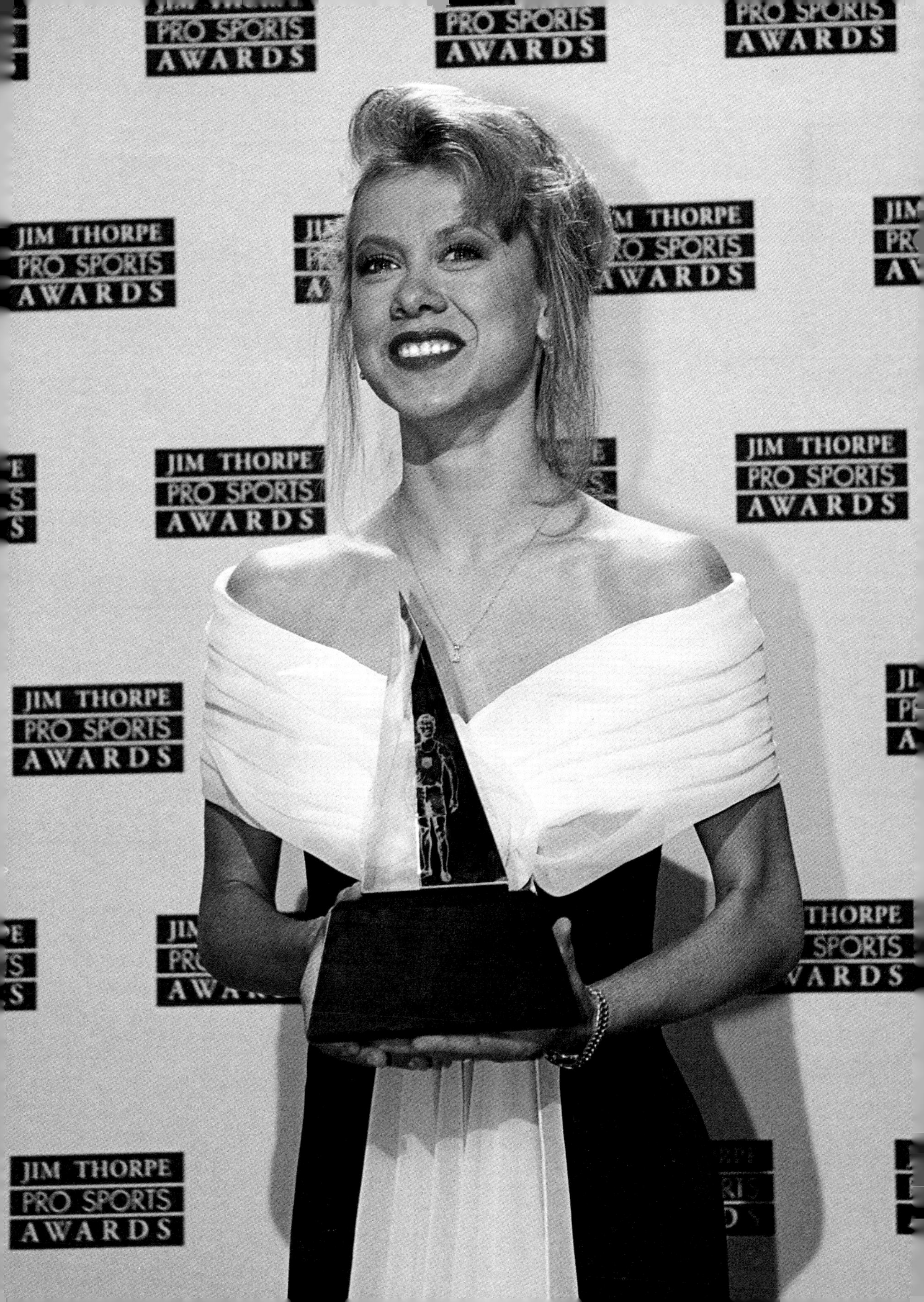
JIM THORPE
PRO SPORTS
AWARDS

ice. "She puts a spell on the judges," said U.S. skater Paul Wylie.

When she finished, Baiul skated off the ice and into the arms of Zmievskaya. While she and her coach waited for the scores, Oksana started to cry. She was thinking of her mother. As her tears flowed, her scores appeared. She had beaten Kerrigan by the smallest of margins—the smallest in Olympic figure skating history. But the scores added up to a gold medal for 16-year-old Oksana Baiul, the little orphan girl from the Ukraine.